Healthcare Analytics 101

A COMPREHENSIVE GUIDE

Sanket Shah

Contents

About the Author

Sanket Shah is a trusted educator in the healthcare industry with expertise in predictive healthcare analytics, business intelligence, and organizational strategy. He has over fifteen years of progressive experience as a strategic thinker with a detailed history of scaling and driving brand positioning for complex HIT solutions across various growth-oriented environments and new and emerging markets.

He's well-networked and has a strong industry reputation and has consistently helped colleagues diversify their revenue streams and adequately address market demand, risk, customer value, and other metrics.

He understands that performance history is directly related to healthcare's most dynamic trends including Data Analytics/BI, care management and coordination, population health management and value-based care, EHR/EMR, HIE, risk profiling, data warehousing, and product development.

The University of Illinois at Chicago Assistant Clinical Professor wanted to make healthcare analytics easier to digest than ever. His new book is particularly well-suited to non-analytically minded professionals. In fact, whether you're new to the healthcare space, or a seasoned pro, you'll receive tangible value from his book, "Healthcare Analytics 101."

Setting the Stage

Organizations in every industry are facing growing concerns over data—and analytics. In healthcare, data is increasing by as much as 48% per year—and approaching the zettabyte and yottabyte scale (the largest prefix in the metric system). Most of that data is unstructured—and considered "dark data."

It's being stored across numerous systems. Various languages and platforms are employed. The point of collection is often lacking and does not account for social, demographic, or other key determinants. It's difficult to find and retain resources to develop and manage analytic solutions. And, as a whole, traditional healthcare has been more reactive versus proactive. It's been more disease-based versus preventative, predictive, and prescriptive. If you thought of an individual's health as a giant tapestry, we're not doing a very good job at painting the entire picture. It's not that the opportunity to fill in the missing information isn't there—because it is. It's staring right back at us.

Enter "Healthcare Analytics 101: A Comprehensive Guide." Whether you're a seasoned pro or a first-year student, this book will help you better understand the current state of healthcare, the "problem" with all the data, and its uses, types, and categories. It also explores an array of next-gen tools and analytic solutions to age-old problems as well as discusses poignant privacy and security concerns as we look ahead. So, without further ado, let's dive right in! Hopefully, as we proceed, we will begin to demystify the entire way people think about analytics.

Chapter 1
Moving the Science Forward

OVERVIEW

T he amount of patient health care data is steadily increasing each year. As healthcare IT expectations continue to evolve, Health Information Exchanges (HIE) are offering secure patient data storage solutions within various care communities throughout the country.

A 2018 report from EMC and the research firm IDC offered a handful of imaginative ways to visualize the health information proliferation; and, per that report, they anticipated an overall increase in health data at a rate increase of 48% each year.[1] Per that same report, they pegged the current volume of healthcare data at 153 exabytes in 2013.

However, that figure had risen exponentially each year and was expected to hit about 2,300 exabytes by the end of 2020. The authors of that report suggest if we stored all of that data on a stack of tablet PCs, in 2013, that stack would have reached about 5,500 miles high. However, only seven short years later, that stack has grown to more than 82,000 miles high, bringing us nearly one-third the way to the moon.

If those growth rates continue—and we have no reason to believe otherwise—then we have a massive, growing problem on our hands (pardon the pun).

In fact, per the above-listed source, healthcare data will soon reach the zettabyte and yottabyte scale. If you were wondering, a zettabyte is equivalent to 152 million years of UHD 8K video format while 1.4 yottabytes is equivalent to the cumulative mass of all the oceans in the world.

Making matters worse, roughly 80% of all that data is unstructured according to numerous estimates. This phenomenon is often referred to as "dark data." For the past several years, healthcare providers have been faced with managing this growing amount of patient medical data along with an increased demand for fast, accurate access to patient records.

To be fair, there are some healthcare organizations that are implementing an array of data-driven solutions that enable these same providers to store and share their data. Later on, we'll discuss a few initiatives underway at the renowned Cleveland Clinic.

From the federal perspective, the US government has incentivized HIE participation, as well, offering states and medical providers grants and loans in hopes to contribute, share, and access data in a secure fashion.

From a clinical perspective, mountains of new data are being produced on a daily basis. Each new clinical trial is designed to answer very specific questions. Even when the answer is "no," there is plenty that can be gleaned from the negative trials, resulting in even further research—and more data.

Traditionally, this data is archived. A researcher moves on to the next big question or the next big trial. But, what if that data (from dozens or hundreds of trials by different companies and/or academic centers) could be shared? If that was something that might help cure cancer, then that's certainly something that we as a society should be doing widespread.

The proper storage and sharing of data is immensely important; and, as you will see, it's a critical component of healthcare analytics and the application of machine learning, which has tremendous implications, many of which we're already starting to see.

There is a treasure trove of information out there, but, currently, most that information is not being utilized to its fullest potential (if at all). For example, most cancer patients enroll in clinical trials for two primary reasons. They want access to new treatments that will benefit their health and help them with their current symptoms. And, they have a vested interest in moving the science forward and helping save the lives of other patients like them.

Unfortunately, the trial system takes so long to test one drug that results often get put on hold for years. Imagine if we pooled all that data to get an inkling of where to go next and determined if there was anything to learn along the way. It's certainly possible. This same concept of data silos and isolated information exists in many healthcare organizations today.

If you were to use that data—regardless of the outcome of the trial, study, or analyses—we would see tremendous implications moving forward. Whether it be from familiar sources such as claims codes and billing data or clinical trials or from emerging sources such as wearable devices and various "omic" sources, each piece of the puzzle needs to come together for a more holistic view of an individual.

Consider the opioid crisis, for example. More and more prescription drug database monitoring programs are being established leading to a better understanding of the epidemic. It's also being used to help prevent abuse by curbing "doctor shopping," for example. Plus, studying the data may help us predict the next big event.

If we look at "Project Data Sphere," we find an even more specific example. The CEO of "Roundtable on Cancer's Life Sciences Consortium" created the independent, non-profit Project

Data Sphere, LLC (PDS) in 2014. The project has been responsible for all aspects of the Project Data Sphere platform, a free digital library-laboratory that is providing one place where the world's research community can share, integrate, and analyze historical, patient-level, comparator-arm data from academic and industry phase III cancer clinical trials.

The platform is available to researchers affiliated with life science companies, hospitals, institutions, and independent researchers. In fact, anyone who is interested in cancer research can become an authorized user through an application process.

The goal of the Project Data Sphere initiative is to ignite innovation that will then help the cancer community unlock the potential of valuable big data by creating all-new insights and opening up new research possibilities that were never before possible.

The true power of the platform is derived from engaging the diverse, global community that's jointly committed to advancing future research and research opportunities in this critical area. I'd even posit that Project Data Sphere may ignite a host of other similar initiatives—but we have not yet seen that materialize.

Let's look at the raw data thus far. Per their main site, data is now freely available, including over 100,000 patients, over 150 datasets, 19,932 downloads, 2,584 users, 35 data providers, and 11,620 logins.[2]

So, not only have they gotten numerous organizations to come to the table and collaborate, just getting them together means that new relationships can be formed which could have tremendous positive long-term value.

The result is that the science can move forward. As such, we need to see a PDS in every major disease category. We need to see that mountain of untapped data be utilized—as well as more collaboration generally.

Data sharing draws attention to connections between different commonly measured things that we would probably never see otherwise. It can change how—and where—we focus our efforts. It pulls together people and groups of people from many different backgrounds, each one bringing a wide range of skills to the table. If they had access to a range of analytics tools and a system to govern and deploy models consistently, they would have more options for solving complex problems.

Chris Donovan, Executive Director of Analytics at Cleveland Clinic noted, "We have employees who are trained in multiple languages and technologies. We want to enable people to access and use languages they're comfortable with but using a common approach."[3]

According to Donovan, Cleveland Clinic hopes to grow analytics maturity across the whole healthcare system. Instead of centralizing analytics skills and capabilities in one team, they're building a broad program across the enterprise. This focus has also helped Cleveland Clinic transform from a focus on disease care to preventive care. Donovan added, "How can we move away from just taking care of you when you show up as an individual patient in the ER or the doctor's office, to looking at a population of patients and thinking about how to prevent people from getting sick in the first place?"

The following four categories are being utilized at Cleveland Clinic—and beyond. Let's look at the following chart then discuss each category of healthcare analytics as we look at how an analytic framework can prove beneficial.[4]

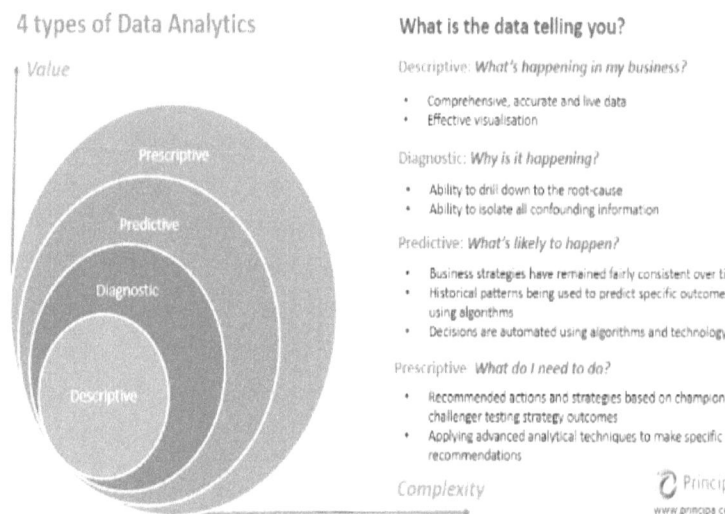

What's happening? Descriptive analytics helps us to define or draw comparisons. It's comprehensive, accurate, and effective. For example, the CFO at a large payer system needs to know his current cost trends over the past three years. An analyst can show a chart with three data points representing each year that will reflect the increase (or decrease) once viewed as a whole. Using this tool, he can define a problem as well as use it to draw comparisons. So, if you're wondering what's happening in your business—descriptive analytics is a great place to start.

Why is it happening? Diagnostic analytics can provide more information and pinpoint certain events. You can isolate information and drill-down to the root cause of an issue. For example, the reason costs are increasing is because knee replacements have been on the rise and the average cost per procedure has jumped 30% per year.

What's likely to happen? Predictive analytics is where we utilize historical and supplemental data to predict what may happen next. Using that data and specific algorithms we can determine the likelihood of a future event. For example, an analyst may determine that based upon the aging population in a given service area plus the increase of medical tourism, costs are likely to continue growing.

What should I do? Prescriptive analytics prescribes a solution to help manage a predicted event. In other words, it involves applying advanced analytic techniques to make more informed decisions. For example, an analyst might conduct some machine-learning algorithmics and identify all patients who underwent a knee replacement and were considered high-risk. He noticed only 20% of them did not have complications, and, of the patients who did not have complications, every one of them underwent weeks of physical therapy both before and after the procedure. Therefore, the analyst was able to recommend suggesting to providers with high-risk knee replacement patients to have them focus on physical therapy before and after the process. Let's now turn to traditional and non-traditional healthcare data uses.

TRADITIONAL VS NON-TRADITIONAL

There are numerous uses for healthcare data, ranging from claims data to electronic records to the input from the Internet of Things like wearables and apps, and more. Healthcare organizations have a whole lot of data and its growing exponentially, as we've noted. The questions are, "What do we do with all of this information?" And "How can we make sense out of it?"

Despite ample security and privacy concerns (many of which we'll cover in subsequent sections), big data is one of the industry's most precious business assets.

For example, providers do not rely on the same information for trimming supply chain costs as they do for identifying diabetics. With each type of information or objective, there's inherently a whole different side of the clinical or administrative functions of the organization.

At the same time, population health management crosses the gap between clinical and financial areas as providers accumulate various categories of data from different sources. For instance, those sources include payers, hospitals, primary care or specialists, pharmacies, public health organizations, and a host of others.

Another example is the explosion of Social Determinants of Health (SDoH) and other publicly available data that can be leveraged to augment existing analytics within an organization. For example, understanding income levels, consumer reported behaviors, or even where an individual lives relative to access to care, grocery stores, or public transit can illuminate how individuals and communities may interact with a healthcare system.

Every piece of information can theoretically contribute to the dimension of a detailed tapestry of a patient's overall health picture, yet, as we know, not all data is of equal value. And, as we've noted, not all data is currently even uniform or accessible. For example, most of the pertinent information for an individual may be found in unstructured, free-text areas within an HER (or "Electronic Health Record").

To mine that information, organizations must leverage tools that deploy natural language processing so that all of that unstructured information can be structured for analytic purposes.

Healthcare organizations who wish to succeed with population health management, quality improvement, and lowering healthcare costs will benefit if they begin shifting their focus on the following types of information.

CLAIMS DATA

Claims data is often considered the starting point for healthcare analytics due to its standardized, structured data format, completeness, and availability.

Claims data includes demographics and other personal info, diagnostics, dates, costs and other billing info, a full range of traditional and non-traditional services (including at-home and ambulatory), all of which help providers process information and understand their patients' basic needs.

Since patients typically use one payer for the vast majority of their health care needs, providers can trust that claims histories will likely represent the entirety of said patients' utilization as long as they are customers of a particular insurance company.

This helps providers bypass interoperability issues that can prevent them from accessing complete and longitudinal clinical data from external organizations.

However, claims codes do have limitations. For example, data is retrospective. It is often months or even years old. Because of this, the lack of up-to-date information can reduce the usefulness of results for proactive populations in terms of their health monitoring or under a preventive model.

Codes do not include an array of valuable clinical details. Plus, they do not directly illuminate the process of care at all, only its more billable aspects.

Does this mean that there are ways to improve current claims systems? Is something more comprehensive possible with the advent of newer technologies? I think you will find that's true.

But let's first discuss the variety and types of records currently available plus the importance of EHR in addressing the previously noted shortfalls of traditional coding data.

EHRs, REGISTRIES & SURVEYS

EHR is an acronym for "Electronic Health Records." EHR data provides many of the clinical clues that claims data leaves out. In addition to all of the information that is coded for reimbursement, EHR contains numerous other details such as the process of care, provider impressions of patients, volunteered patient concerns, and more. They also include vital signs, medications, allergies, imaging reports, lab data, and immunization dates.

With these datasets, providers can answer a wealth of important population health management questions. For example, which patients have blood pressure readings that have been trending up? How many patients are taking multiple medications at one time? Can these be reduced? Which diabetics have missed their latest eye health screenings? How many patients are using tobacco or vaping? And, have they been offered access to smoking-cessation resources?

Health surveys and disease registries are other examples.[5] Disease registries are clinical information systems that track a narrow range of key data for certain chronic conditions such as Alzheimer's, cancer, diabetes, heart disease, asthma, and more. Disease registries are providing important information for managing a range of patient conditions. Let's look at a few of the major disease registries.

GAAIN is the "Global Alzheimer's Association Interactive Network." The Global Alzheimer's Association Interactive Network is a collaborative project that provides researchers around the world access to a large vault of Alzheimer's disease data and sophisticated analytical tools to work with the data.

The National Cardiovascular Data Registry (or "NCDR") is a global suite of data registries that assists hospitals and private entities to improve the quality of cardiovascular care being provided.

The National Trauma Data Bank (or "NTDB") is the largest aggregation of trauma registry ever assembled. The goal of the NTDB is to inform the medical community, the public, and decision-makers about a whole host of issues that characterize the current state of care for injured patients.

The Medicare Current Beneficiary Survey (or "MCBS") is a continuous, multipurpose survey of a nationally representative sample of the Medicare population. Its stated goals are to determine expenditures and sources of payment for all services used by Medicare beneficiaries.

The Medical Expenditure Panel Survey (MEPS) is a set of large-scale surveys of families and individuals, their medical providers, and employers across the United States. MEPS is the most complete source of data on the cost and use of health care and health insurance coverage.

This is just a small sample of surveys and registries. Refer to the aforementioned endnote for more examples.

In terms of EHRs, they also have downsides, as well. They may include free-text fields, meaning they are filled with unstructured data, and that unstructured data can sometimes be incomplete or hard to analyze.

Or, on the opposite end, EHRs often have drop-downs with pre-populated fields that, in many cases, do not provide a selection that accurately represents a patient's current situation. Often times, providers are "stuck" with their choices and will try and make the best choice available.

Similarly, there are too many choices or "clicks" to make. These fields, in many cases considered analytically relevant, often go unpopulated based on data-entry fatigue.

Unintuitive options encourage users to take shortcuts, copy and paste data from their visit, and, often, incorrectly enter values, thus further weakening the integrity of data collected.

Also, EHRs sometimes store results such as imaging reports and notes from specialists (as static PDF files) that can't be analyzed without additional processing. Some filters actually view PDF's like images—and cannot analyze the content adequately. There are numerous shortfalls, but the positives outweigh the negatives, and EHRs are a step in the right direction.

In one recent survey, close to 40% of stakeholders are making EHR optimization a top budget priority over the next three years.[6] According to that source, over 20% of stakeholders also plan to focus specifically on accountable care and population health management technology improvements.

SOCIAL DETERMINANTS

Socioeconomic data and information about the social determinants of health are important resources to examine. However, a lot of that data goes entirely uncollected or gets scattered in inaccessible formats and is completely wasted.

Just imagine how valuable social and community determinant information would be if we could properly harness it. Take for instance community traits such as average incomes, language proficiency, local food choices, violence, transportation, unemployment, and educational factors, all of which could be important predictors of future patient outcomes.

As previously noted, HER fields are very limiting. For instance, they do not (typically) allow providers to collect information on social determinants at the point of care. And when that data is available, interoperability barriers or simply getting publicly available information integrated within their existing systems prevents providers from accessing it.

Claims data and classifications have started to enable some capturing of social determinant data via ICD-10-CM codes included in categories Z55-Z65 ("Z codes"), which identify non-medical factors that may influence a patient's health status.

Existing Z codes identify issues related to a patient's socioeconomic situation, including education and literacy, employment, housing, lack of adequate food or water or occupational exposure to risk factors like dust, radiation, or toxic agents. However, most coders or providers are still unfamiliar with this coding inclusion and thus the data is not quite reliable as of today.

Furthermore, without environmental as well as social and community data, providers are totally unable to paint a full tapestry of a person's health care concern. As a result, healthcare organizations aren't able to develop population health management programs to address the total array of their patients' health care needs.

In November 2016, CMS detailed their aptly named "Equity Plan for Improving Quality in Medicare," which prioritizes the collection and analysis of social determinants of health.[7] Other initiatives from payers, providers, and academic researchers have resulted in interactive dashboards outlining community challenges, such as interpersonal violence, drug usage, economic disparities, and other determinants at the state, county, and city levels where patients reside.

CONSUMER DATA

One example of consumer data is in Patient Generated Health Data (PGHD), which takes many forms.

PGHDs can include satisfaction surveys, patient-reported outcomes (PROs), communications via portable, data streaming devices, fitness trackers, mobile apps (mHealth) and other Internet of Things (IoT) devices.

The overall interest in personalized healthcare is surging in recent years along with the wider spread adoption of wearables and IoT devices. Of course, if the information is unstructured and siloed by various point solution vendors, institutions, or entities, it's still not being shared.

Invariably, it's difficult to utilize largely unstructured datasets because the sheer volume of available information can be off-putting. Plus, providers often question how to even integrate an endless stream of real-time IoT data into their existing workflows.

High-risk patients benefit most from around-the-clock, real-time monitoring, but most individuals do not require constant attention to their particulars such as sleep patterns, heart data, and exercise regimes to stay healthy.

EHR developers are beginning to work on innovative ways to integrate PGHD and constant, real-time alerting into their products. And, ultimately, having intuitive, streamlined data combed into the overall workflow in clinical, end-user environments will be critical for ensuring IoT data doesn't overwhelm providers on a daily basis.

However, data analytics teams are taking a broader view of population health. For instance, mHealth apps that collect PGHD about lifestyle and mental health issues are beginning to demonstrate their worth at increasing wellnesses, adherence rates, and informing providers about the increased need for targeted intervention.

Concurrently, EHRs and claims data contain information on which medications are prescribed, and the rise in e-prescribing is making even more digital data available for analytics.

But on their own, none of these sources can follow-up with whether patients fill their prescriptions regularly or take their medications as prescribed.

Medication adherence data is really an amalgamation of several of the aforementioned data types, namely socioeconomic data, prescription and/or pharmacy issues, educational data, patient-generated responses to prescribed therapies, prescription rates, associated diagnoses, and more.[8]

At the end of the day, the data can be considered held hostage by those that "own" the information. Although there are conversations at Capitol Hill and CMS as to who really owns the patient record, for the time being, we have various stakeholders which creates a challenge for sharing and transparency.

The industry is still developing tools to combine all these disparate data types reliably concerning risk scoring, population assessment, and targeted intervention. To leverage that data alongside other types of available information, healthcare organizations must begin investing in comprehensive population health management solutions to generate actionable insights from multiple data sources.

PLATFORMS & LANGUAGES

Currently, there are varying debates between source systems, so many analytics are focusing on the modeling itself. Open platforms allow stakeholders to employ code data, leverage open

23

source opportunities, and, in some cases, open things up to all new code sets.

The ability to integrate disparate code, processes, and information into one hub provides consistent delivery of information. Popular languages include SQL, Python, Ruby on Rails, and SAS. It's outside our purview to investigate each language in detail—but we do provide examples.

More and more people are coding across multiple interfaces using different ways to collaborate on modeling initiatives. There are varying ways to publish or demonstrate output deployment and models. We do know that SAS allows programmers and others to effectively bring everything together in previously unforeseen ways.

SAS is an acronym standing for "Statistical Analysis System," which was first developed by NC State University from 1966 until 1976 and was further developed by the SAS Institute in the 1980s and 1990s. SAS enables predictive analytics in healthcare and other industries as well as an array of other applications beyond our industry.

As noted earlier, one such example of predictive analytics in healthcare today is occurring at Cleveland Clinic. According to US News & World Reports, Cleveland Clinics is ranked No. 4 on the Best Hospitals Honor Roll. It's also rated high-performing in 9 adult procedures and conditions.[9]

Cleveland Clinic is a teaching hospital and is at the forefront of healthcare data and analytics. For them, giving more people access to analytics is not seen as a liability but as an opportunity. Beyond data scientists and programmers who are adept at writing code and creating advanced analytics, leaders at Cleveland Clinic want to make data more easily available to both executives and managers with high-end end-user interfaces and drag-and-drop capabilities. That means you don't have to be incredibly computer or code-savvy to operate many of the solutions they're addressing. The shift in business intelligence over the past decade or so has moved from very specialized skills to create basic reporting to a more self-service approach where tools are intuitive, and reporting is much more attainable enterprise-wide.

Chris Donovan, Executive Director of Analytics at Cleveland Clinic, recently said, "Our leaders may not know how to build a predictive model, but they need to be able to use data to make better decisions. Not everyone is a data scientist. But everyone needs to be able to interact with data at their level."[10]

Donovan also suggested that Cleveland Clinic is redefining what an analyst is and working on ways to create a common entry point for all levels of users. As you can see, for Cleveland Clinic, broadening the use of analytics to support all users is more than a technology tactic, It's a business strategy. "Analytics is not just a capability that supports your core strategy," Donovan added. "It has to be a core strategy of its own. You need to become an analytically mature organization, and you need to be world-class in that space or people will leapfrog you."

For most healthcare organizations, there can be a plethora of tools and platforms available for data mining and analytic exercises. One must fully understand the underlying data architecture to begin providing meaningful analytics.

As with the following chart, start with the foundational raw data, access it through programming languages, run machine-learning scripts and ultimately present the information (the idea is to familiarize yourself with how data flows through your organization for improved analytics).[11]

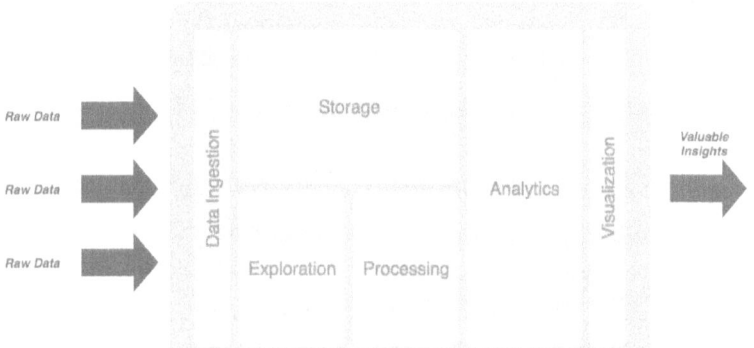

CODED DATA

Of course, collecting health information is nothing new. People have been collecting healthcare and disease data for hundreds of years. For example, per our source, a "Weekly Bill of Mortality" was established in London, England, in 1634.[12]

Per that source, the coding of diagnostic information began in the 1850s and was focused on capturing information related to death. At that time, a classification known as "The International List of Causes of Death" was first developed. The method of capturing mortality information was later adopted by the International Statistical Institute in 1893.

Then, much later, WHO took over the responsibility for the International Classification of Diseases (ICD) in 1948, and the classification was expanded to include morbidity (diseases and conditions affecting the patient). Following that, in 1967, the World Health Assembly adopted the use of the ICD, for use of mortality and morbidity statistics for all member states. Let's discuss ICD and then move on to a more comprehensive discussion of coding data and sets (follow-up with full definitions in our appendix).

ICD stands for the "International Classifications of Diseases," and it is the international standard diagnostic classification for general epidemiological, health management, and clinical uses.

Coded data as a whole is used for the analysis of general health situations of population groups, and for monitoring the incidence frequency and prevalence of diseases and other health problems. Using coded data, it's possible for analysts to study the characteristics and circumstances of individuals affected and make broad-sweeping predictions in many cases.

The data can be used for reimbursement applications, resource allocation, quality assessment, clinical guidelines, and more. Coded data also provides a basis for the compilation of national mortality and morbidity statistics for WHO member states.

Once collected, ICD data is used by various healthcare providers and decision-makers to monitor the health of individuals and populations. That data can also be used for the analysis of the entire health system or individual patients. Uses include but is not limited to hospitals, healthcare practitioners, government, professional associations, researchers, epidemiologists, academia (professors and students), and the general public.

Some of the specific ways coded data is used includes disease trending by demographic group or geographic area, disease registries, cause-of-death statistics, surveillance, hospital utilization, injury statistics, evaluation of healthcare and public health interventions, identifying types of healthcare services provided to specific patient groups, determining the overall health of the population, human resource issues related to the delivery of healthcare, reimbursement strategies through insurance companies or government, and more.

There are numerous types and grains of healthcare data available and this section serves as a general overview of pertinent healthcare data codes.

Furthermore, codes covered herein are used in HIPAA named transactions and are external to the transaction implementation guides maintained separately from various individual standards.

ICD-10 is the tenth revision of the International Statistical Classification of Diseases and Related Health Problems. The World Health Organization (WHO) manages the base code set; WHO members including the United States have modified the list to meet their needs.

Per our source, the Department of Health and Human Services (HHS) published the "HIPAA Administrative Simplification: Modifications to Medical Data Code Set Standards to Adopt ICD–10–CM and ICD–10–PCS Final Rule" on January 16, 2009, which required healthcare providers and health plans to utilize ICD-10-CM diagnosis codes and ICD-10-PCS inpatient procedure codes for dates of service or discharge on or after October 1, 2013.[13]

Per that same source, in August 2014, HHS published its final extension in the "Administrative Simplification: Change to the Compliance Date for the International Classification of Diseases, 10th Revision (ICD-10-CM and ICD-10-PCS) Medical Data Code Sets Final Rule," which set the compliance date to October 1, 2015.

The following codes come from that same source (referenced in the appendix). Claim Adjustment Reason Codes (CARC) describe the reason for a payment adjustment relating to the adjudication of a healthcare claim. CARC codes are maintained by the Codes Maintenance Committee and maintained three times per year (e.g., February, June, and October).

Code on Dental Procedures and Nomenclature (CDT) codes are used to document dental treatment. CDT code set has been named as a HIPAA standard. CDT codes are maintained by the American Dental Association (ADA) and maintained once per year in January.

Current Procedural Terminology (CPT) codes are used for coding professional (physician and outpatient) procedures. The CPT code set has been named as a HIPAA standard, and they are maintained by the American Medical Association (AMA) and maintained once per year in January.

Claim Status Category Codes describe the general category of a claim's status (accepted, rejected, etc.). These codes are maintained by the Codes Maintenance Committee and maintained three times per year in February, June, and October.

ICD-10-CM refers to the International Classification of Diseases (10TH Revision) Clinical Modification. ICD-10-CM is the clinical modification of the World Health Organization's ICD-10 diagnosis codes.

The ICD-10-CM has been named as a HIPAA standard, replacing ICD-9 for all claims with dates of service on and after 10/1/2015 or for inpatient claims, with a date of discharge of 10/1/2015 or later. ICD-10-CM codes are maintained by the National Center for Health Statistics (NCHS) and maintained once per year in October.

ICD-10-PCS refers to the International Classification of Diseases (10th Revision) Procedure Coding System. ICD-10-PCS is the United States' clinical modification of the World Health Organization's ICD-10 procedure coding system and is used for coding hospital inpatient procedures.

The ICD-10-PCS code set has been named as a HIPAA standard, replacing ICD-9 for all claims with dates of service on and after 10/1/2015 or for inpatient claims, with a date of discharge of 10/1/2015 or later. ICD-10-PCS codes are maintained by the Centers for Medicare & Medicaid Services (CMS) and maintained once per year in October.

Healthcare Common Procedure Coding System (HCPCS) is used primarily to identify products, supplies, and services not included in the CPT code set, such as durable medical equipment, prosthetics, and ambulance services. HCPCS has been named as a HIPAA standard. HCPS is maintained by the Centers for Medicare & Medicaid Services (CMS) and updated once per year in January (although quarterly updates are done when necessary).

Healthcare Provider Taxonomy Codes (HPTC) categorize the type, classification, and/or specialization of healthcare providers. They are maintained by the National Uniform Claim Committee (NUCC) and released twice per year in July and January.

Healthcare Review Decision Reason Codes (HRDRC) codes describe the reason for the health service review outcome. They are maintained by the Codes Maintenance Committee. They are updated three times per year (February, June, and October).

Logical Observation Identifiers Names and Codes (LOINC) is a universal standard used to assist in the electronic exchange and gathering of clinical information. They are maintained by the Regenstrief Institute.

National Drug Codes (NDC) identify the vendor (manufacturer), product and package size of all drugs and biologics recognized by the FDA. They are maintained by the U. S. Food and Drug Administration (FDA) and scheduled for daily maintenance.

National Uniform Billing Committee (NUBC) code sets consist of the following grains of data/codes and are used in or relating to healthcare claims.

Type of Bill Codes is the type of facility and classification of the claim. Type of Bill Frequency Codes represents a sequence of a claim in the current episode of institutional care (e.g., admit through discharge, interim billing, etc.). Priority (Type) of Admission Visit Codes describe the priority of admission (e.g., emergency, urgent, etc.). Point of Origin of Admission or Visit Codes describe where admissions or visits originated from. Patient Discharge Status Codes explain the disposition or discharge status of the patient at the point of billing. Condition Codes explain conditions or events that may affect the processing of the claim. Occurrence Codes describe single occurrence dates used in the claim.

Occurrence Span Codes describe date spans used in the claim. Value Codes describe values significant to the processing of a claim. And, Revenue Codes identify accommodations, ancillary services, unique billing calculations, or arrangements relevant to the claim.

Also, NUBC Codes are maintained by the NUBC, and those codes are scheduled for maintenance three times per year (e.g., January, April, and July).

Place of Service Codes (PSC) describe the location where a service is rendered. These codes are maintained by the Centers for Medicare and Medicaid Services (CMS). There is no fixed schedule for this code set.

Lastly, Remittance Advice Remark Codes (RARC) are used to further describe (in addition to the Claim Adjustment Reason Codes) the reason for an adjustment to claim payment or to or convey information about remittance processing. RARC Codes are maintained by the Centers for Medicare & Medicaid Services (CMS). They are updated or serviced three times per year (March, July, and November). All these codes are listed alphabetically in our appendix for additional resources. Let's also discuss key changes in the codes themselves plus implementation.

ANALYTIC APPLICATIONS

Codes and datasets can be leveraged to understand an individual, a group, or even a specific cohort. Traditionally, these codes and other financials may be found on healthcare claims which contain other pertinent information. For analytic exercises, a person may begin to use claims data to define the category of service. In other words, determining if a claim is generated out of the professional side (often referred to as the physician claim), the inpatient setting, the outpatient or facility setting, or if the claim is a pharmacy claim.

Furthermore, claims data can be enriched or enhanced through various groupers. One common grouping is bundling or "stitching" together clinically related events as an episode. *Episodes* contain a series of claims, clinical, and non-traditional data to better understand the health status of an individual or cost of a condition.

Coded data can also be enhanced by third-party risk assessment and scoring software. For example, taking demographics, history, diagnostic related groupings (DRG) and a comparative benchmark, a risk score can be generated and leveraged to better understand concurrent and prospective costs for an individual.

IMPORTANT CHANGES

There are continuous changes to the aforementioned codes. Until recently, reimbursement for remote patient monitoring services was a gray area for providers. It was only recently that CMS issued its final 2019 Physician Fee Schedule and Quality Payment Program, which opened the door to reimbursement of services that enable providers to manage and coordinate care from home.

There were a number of other changes, as well. For example, there's been a wider scale implementation of new CPT codes. Specifically, CPT code 99453 sets parameters on remote monitoring regarding measuring weight, blood pressure, pulse oximetry, and respiratory flow rate, as well as guidelines on patient education surrounding such equipment. Also, PT code 99454 is similar to 99453 but focuses on the devices themselves and sets guidelines around daily recordings and programmed alerts.

The most impactful new CPT code for providers, according to our source, is CPT 99457. That's where the reimbursement picture becomes a little clearer.

CPT code 99547 went live in January 2018, and it offered Medicare reimbursement for remote physiologic monitoring treatment management services, plus twenty minutes or more of clinical staff, physician, or other qualified healthcare professional's time in a calendar month that required interactive communication with the patient and/ or caregiver.

When CMS's final rule was published late-2018, CMS said code 99457 described professional's time, meaning it could not be furnished auxiliary personnel to a practitioner's professional services. But in a technical correction inspired by industry feedback, CMS removed that sentence entirely and confirmed that those services could be furnished by auxiliary personnel incident to a practitioner's professional service.

The change means that remote patient services (such as Telehealth) are now more closely aligned with chronic care management services, the difference being that the default rule for incident-to billing under Medicare requires direct supervision.

Direct supervision means a physician and all auxiliary personnel have to be in the same building at the same time, though not necessarily in the same room. Whereas, general supervision, on the other hand, doesn't require all parties to be in the same building simultaneously. Instead, the physician could use telemedicine to facilitate general supervision over the auxiliary personnel, and those new code changes reflect (seemingly to the applauds of Telehealth and other remote practitioners).

REVIEW & REFLECT

At the end of the day, it doesn't matter how much data you have. If that data isn't uniform, isn't stored properly, or isn't readily accessible, it will remain what's called "dark data." That means it's doing no one any good. In fact, it's causing major problems.

As noted, each year we're adding approximately 48% more data while as much as 80% of that data is unusable to analytics (at least previously).

While there are pioneers at Cleveland Clinic, widespread analytics opportunities aren't being met. Yet, as we know, everyone is a patient at some time or another during their life, and we all want good medical care.

However, we assume that doctors are all medical experts and that there is good research behind all their decisions. While that's mostly true, I don't think it paints a complete picture, at least so far as big data is concerned. That data represents mountains of valuable insights into patients' needs.

Physicians are smart, well trained and do their best to stay up to date with the latest research. But they can't possibly commit to memory all the knowledge they need for every situation, and they probably don't have it all at their fingertips. I think we need to do something about that.

Even if they did have access to the massive amounts of data needed to compare treatment outcomes for all the diseases they encounter, they would still need time and expertise to analyze that information and integrate it with the patient's own medical profile. But this kind of in-depth research and statistical analysis is beyond the scope of a physician's work. That's why more physicians (and insurance companies) are using predictive analytics to make things easier than before.

Accordingly, we begin shifting away from the issue of data (it's uses, types, codes, languages, platforms, etc.) and begin focusing on ways to take that data and leverage it for all the valuable insights it entails.

Chapter 2

Predictive Analytics

P redictive analytics (PA) uses technology and various statistical methodologies to proactively sift through massive amounts of information, analyze and extrapolate that information, and attempt to predict outcomes for individual patients. It takes, in many cases, traditional means of data plus non-traditional means to put more tools in practitioners' hands than ever before.

In medicine, those predictions can range. Responses to medications to hospital readmission rates and much more are included. Then, predictions are made using that data. For example, predicting infections, methods of suturing, determining the likelihood of disease, helping a physician treat or diagnosis, and even predicting future wellness. All this and so much more can be done with predictive analytics.

The statistical methods are called learning models because they can grow in precision with additional cases. There are two major ways in which PA differs from traditional statistics (and from evidence-based medicine). First, predictions are made for individuals, not groups. Second, predictive analytics does not rely upon a normal (bell-shaped) curve.

Prediction modeling uses concepts such as artificial intelligence or marching learning to create a prediction profile using algorithms and information from past individuals. The model is then deployed, so that a new individual can get a prediction instantly for whatever their need is, whether that's for an accurate diagnosis or how healthy (or unhealthy) a person will be in say 1 year, 5 years, or 20 years.

There are numerous benefits of PA in medicine, too many to adequately address herein. However, we'll cover six of the major benefits of PA as it relates to the healthcare industry.

BENEFITS OF PREDICTIVE ANALYTICS

For starters, under the Affordable Care Act (popularly known as the "ACA" or "Obamacare"), one of its first mandates was within what's called "Meaningful Use," which dictates that patients cannot be readmitted before thirty days of being dismissed from a hospital.

For some background, the Affordable Care Act (ACA) was the comprehensive health care reform law enacted in March 2010; and, it had three primary goals above others.[14] Those goals were to make affordable health insurance available to more people, provide consumers with subsidies (or "premium tax credits") that lower costs for households with incomes between 100% and 400% of the federal poverty level, and expand Medicaid to cover all adults with incomes below 138% of poverty (note, not all states have expanded their Medicaid programs), and support innovative medical care delivery methods designed to lower the costs of health care.

Due to the changes (note, the individual mandate has been lifted since that time but most of the particulars of the ACA remain intact), hospitals needed predictive models to accurately assess when a patient could safely be released.

Next, predictive analytics will increase the accuracy of a physicians' diagnosis. Practitioners can use predictive algorithms to help them make more informed decisions as well as more targeted, more accurate diagnoses in many cases. For example, when patients come to the ER with chest pain, it is often difficult to know whether the patient should be hospitalized. But if a doctor could answer questions about that patient and her condition along with a tested and accurate predictive algorithm, it would assess the likelihood the patient could be sent home safely, plus weight that against their own clinical judgment. The prediction would not replace those judgments under this model, but it would go a long way toward ensuring physicians make the most informed decisions possible.

In a visit to one's primary care physician, the following might occur. The doctor has been following a patient for many years. The patient's genome includes a gene marker for early-onset Alzheimer's disease, determined by researchers using predictive analytics. This gene is rare and runs in the patient's family on one side. Several years ago, when it was first discovered, the patient agreed to have his blood taken to see if he had the gene. After learning he did, he also learned that there was no gene treatment available. However, evidence-based research indicated that PCP conditions may be helpful for many early Alzheimer's patients. As such, the doctor's advice has been augmented by PA and big data.

Next, PA can help preventive medicine and public health in terms of early intervention efforts. With earlier intervention, many diseases can be entirely prevented if not ameliorated, not unlike what happened with the advent and wide-spread implementation of vaccines.

Plus, when a patient receives that information, they themselves can make better life and health decisions. It's the gift that keeps on giving with numerous positive reverberations. As patients' health increases, the overall health of a population increases, as well, saving untold amounts of money in an industry plagued with hyperinflating costs otherwise. Again, when you think data think opportunity and those opportunities include more than just the obvious health considerations.

As we know, throughout the history of practiced medicine, we've been far too consumed by sick-care versus having the luxury of acting proactively. We have traditionally waited until a person was sick then set about targeting the symptoms and not the underlying causes. Now, PA has the ability to help people sort out what works for them by looking at similar subtypes and seeking help for patterns of responses.

Something called EBM or Evidence Based Medicine is a big step in the right direction as we move forward. It's providing more help with simple hunches and helping practitioners determine what works best for the middle of a normal distribution of people.

Of course, we know that this approach has drawbacks, as what's good for a middle/average group of people won't always translate into what's best for an individual, but, again, it's a step in the right direction.

It's all about augmenting the physician, not replacing the physician, which brings me to my next point about—PA is providing doctors with answers they need from individuals patients. Think about this.

It can prove dangerous to give treatments to the wrong person or something that we knowingly won't work specifically for them. So, better, more accurate diagnoses of the problem along with targeted treatment are what's needed. To that end, PA is providing employers and hospitals with an array of predictions concerning insurance costs. Under the ACA, employers were tasked with providing healthcare insurance for their employees. Those same employers can now input certain characteristics of their workforce into predictive analytic algorithms and obtain predictions about their future medical costs.

What's more, what if they combed those predictions into their own data? The implications are limitless, whether it's a business that barely meets the minimum threshold of fifty employees under the ACA or it's a large conglomerate like Walmart with thousands of employees spanning US (and certain other countries).

Some of this is beyond our scope, but I would add that employers could also use PA to determine what providers were giving them the most effective products for their particular needs. That info could be built into the new models and to discover if an average employee visits a primary care physician a certain amount of time per year and that could determine particular rates and premiums, for example. Again, the opportunities are limitless, which is a testament to the capabilities imaginable with PA.

Or, for example, hospitals could work with insurance providers as they seek to optimize particular outcomes or the quality assurance needed to maintain their accreditation. In tailoring treatments that produce better outcomes, accreditation standards are documented and increasingly met over time using valuable nuggets of information that was previously be squandered altogether, if even collected in the first place.

PA has the ability to shed light on things that we've never seen before and this is particularly true in the healthcare industry. It's impossible to adequately define precisely what those possibilities may entail, but let's just say that PA is continuously bringing our attention and focus onto things that were not always focused on before, which is leading to more innovation, as well.

PA also allows researchers to use predictive models that don't require thousands of cases or they become more and more accurate over time. In terms of large population studies, very small incremental differences can prove to be statistically significant, as researchers are uncovering that randomly assigned case-control studies are far superior to traditional observational studies.

We also know that PA models can be generated with small numbers of cases and the data and feedback improves over time with each subsequent case. In this sense, the modeling has come alive and is actively leaning, adapting, adding new information, and making changes along the way, changes that are reflective in the population being studied.

To take advantage of those practices, electronic data record systems need to become more compatible with one another, and that takes us back to a problem we've broached time and again throughout this inquiry (i.e., the lack of uniformity, something that must be addressed sooner rather than later).

One way to create data that's more uniform and more broadly usable is by way of governing authorities. These systems will require further transparency and accountability, but I advise to keep in mind what the goals are—reducing costs and improving quality of care and overall health. If that's the goal, then anything is possible if the collective will be there.

As we move forward, physician roles will perhaps need to change more, as well, from more of a consultant versus a decision-maker, someone who advises and warns and thereby helps individual patients using the best information and predictive analytics available.

To those ends, let's look at some of the more advanced ways PA is infiltrating the current healthcare industry. As you will note, these changes can literally revolutionize the entire way that medicine is practiced throughout the world for better health and disease reductions and improved health overall. Keep in mind, this is NOT an endorsement of any particular software or company.

DISRUPTING AN INDUSTRY

As I know first-hand, the whole healthcare industry is ripe for disruption by way of AI and machine learning and predictive analytics as a whole. According to this source, Accenture estimates that AI in healthcare will reach $6.6 billion by the end of 2020.[15]

Numerous companies are starting to assist hospitals, insurers, and other stakeholders in various aspects of predictive modeling. As part of the scope of this book, for instance, I researched the use of predictive analytics in healthcare to help me better understand where AI is coming into play.

Several important questions would come to mind. Namely, what are some of the types of PA applications currently in use in healthcare? Or, what are some of the tangible results of that PA? And, are there any common trends amongst those innovative efforts? If so, how might those trends affect the future of the healthcare industry as well as individual health and population health?

Per the previously listed source, insurance providers can use an HCC Profiler to predict the commercial risk of health plans listed on ACA exchanges. For more information on that tool, please refer to this endnote.[16]

According to the company that makes the product, insurance providers can use their HCC Profiler tool to predict the commercial risk of health plans they list on ACA health insurance exchanges. The software can potentially analyze data from patient records and medical billing statements as well as provide health insurers listing certain plans with an overall risk score for those plans. The company claims this could allow health insurers to better predict the costs of offering their health insurance plans and the success they might have on ACA exchanges.

However, it is unclear if Apixio is currently selling to any prominent hospital systems or insurance agencies nor any evidence that their executives have robust academic or professional experience in AI. More information would be required.

However, they do claim that hospital coders can be uploaded from a hospital or provider's EHR or from image scans or PDFs of patient records into their "HCC Profiler system." Then, HCC Profiler seems to mine the patient record data for relevant information, including blood pressure, diagnoses, and the drugs the patient was prescribed or administered during their stay at the hospital. Hospital coders add and designate codes based on the diagnoses and demographic data in a patient's medical records, which is used to determine how much an insurance company owes a hospital.

There are numerous other technologies being deployed as well. These may prove impactful moving forward. In general, machine learning refers to high-quality data being accurately mined by high-end computers that "learn" based on previous inputs.

We cannot say for sure about Apixio's profiler, but, generally speaking, an algorithm's pattern-recognition capabilities, can be used to draw-out previously unrevealed correlations that can improve how doctor's interact with patients, diagnose illnesses, and prescribe medications (when necessary).

Machine learning has the opportunity to dramatically reshape the entire way healthcare is administered in this country—and beyond, particularly as we see more collaboration between for-profits.

While in the long run, it may prove possible to use the complexity of this type of predictive analytics to forewarn patients and pre-treat illnesses, these issues are still inadequately understood. However, as it relates to dementia, for example, analytics is already being put to predictive use with fantastic results. There are other such efforts happening, as well.

For example, the four hospitals of the Assistance Publique-Hôpitaux de Paris are crunching numbers and giving hourly predictions of expected admission levels. Also, per our source, in this country, Carnegie Mellon and Pittsburgh universities' aptly named "Big Data for Better Health Project" is using a supercomputer to analyze and model incredibly large volumes of complex data on cancer patients, producing more accurate predictions than was previously.

Not to mention, San Francisco-based healthcare provider Dignity Health is using analytics to pioneer what it calls a "bio-surveillance" system to generate high-probability, real-time alerts for patients and doctors.[17]

Per that source, their system allows clinicians to head-off sepsis, a deadly type of infection affecting 6% of patients admitted to hospitals in the US alone. Sepsis also carries a high risk of mortality (e.g., from 25-50% based on severity). There are also a number of breakthroughs in wearable technologies.

WEARABLES & OTHER TECH

Healthcare is getting more access to patient information than ever before, especially with the advent of wearable, IoT or IoT-like devices and apps. These devices help us receive and process patient information in ways never before possible.

In fact, the proliferation of wearables such as Fitbit to an array of FDA-approved devices demonstrates the disruptive nature of the new technology. According to our source, the global market for medical wearable devices will reach $12.1 billion by the end of the calendar year 2020, and the U.S. is representing the largest percentage of that market in the world driven by breakthroughs and investments in and around Silicon Valley.[18]

Wearable devices can be used to track a runner's vital signs or health and fitness-related data, location, etc., for example (also see our *Case Study* subsequently). The healthcare space is going through a digital revolution with the invasion of such technologies led by medical wearables with artificial intelligence and big data which are providing new, additional value to a healthcare industry struggling otherwise with preventative health.

Wearable devices applied to healthcare offer multiple advantages to healthcare professionals and patients including personalization, early diagnosis, remote patient monitoring, adherence to medication, and information registration all of which lead to optimum decision-making by doctors and significant savings in healthcare costs.

In terms of personalization, we know that the doctor, with the help of the device, can quickly create a program based on the exact needs of the patient. As for early diagnosis, we know that precise medical parameters in wearable devices allow early detection of symptoms which can lead to root causes being explored.

Healthcare professionals can also monitor patients remotely and in real-time through the use of wearable devices. They can ensure that patients are adhering to their medication or other advice.

For the patients, wearable devices help ensure that they're taking their medications on time. The patient's medical doctor can then be informed that they're adhering to those prescriptions in terms of dose and frequency.

In terms of information registry, the data stored allows for a more exhaustive analysis of any information collected. Of course, all this leads to optimum decisions by doctors as well as the potential for significant savings in healthcare costs. To illustrate all this better, let's take a look at our case study.

CASE STUDY

Let's envision a hypothetical system called PROJECT STATISTICA that takes real-time, real-world data from patients via wearables along with a detailed intake questionnaire plus follow-up information from their providers where possible. Under this scenario, our patient is named Xavier (or "Patient X," for short).

Patient X is 45-years-old. He only sees his primary care provider about once per year for check-ups, physicals, the occasional cold or stuffy nose, and that sort of thing. For the most part, he seems healthy. He exercises three times per week. His wife recently advised utilizing an IoT wearable that would provide feedback and monitor his heart. She also heard about PROJECT STATISTICA and was fascinated by the possibilities.

Reluctantly, Patient X wears his device while exercising. In his questionnaire, he noted that his father had heart disease at a young age. He noted an array of other personal questions plus questions related to his social status (income, social determinants, etc.).

He became used to wearing the device over time, and, unbeknownst to him, a lot of data was being collected. Analysts with PROJECT STATISTICA were studying his information augmented by AI and advanced algorithms. They were able to deduce that Xavier was 35% more susceptible to heart attack than other patients his age.

They alerted the patient, and he quickly followed up with his doctor. Xavier's records were reviewed including everything compiled by PROJECT STATISTICA, and with all the additional information available, his doctor was able to concur. He took everything he already knew and weighted it against other patients of similar demographics and background plus the new data collected, which all led him to believe that the patient's chance of heart attack was indeed much more significant than others.

As such, a whole new lifestyle regimen was prescribed along with a small dose aspirin. More time came and went—and Xavier lived a long, fulfilling life for many years to come, never suffering from heart attack as his father once did.

Note, while this case study is purely hypothetical, given the advent of new technologies, many of which we've already covered in greater detail, we know that what happened to Xavier is *possible*. But it's completely fictional at the same time and only used to demonstrate a certain range of possibilities.

Remember to not take this case study, this book, or any portion of this book as specific medical advice. Please consult a trained doctor or qualified healthcare provider before initiating any new medical treatments or lifestyle changes. And, as always, if you're in a life-threatening situation contact a healthcare provider immediately. Our book is purely meant for educational purposes only.

As we look to the years ahead (as more and more info is collected), the need for security and privacy is exacerbated by the amassing mountains of data. As such, regulations are constantly changing, as well, and no discussion on analytics in healthcare would be complete without discussing HIPAA and other security and privacy considerations, as well. So, let's briefly review those considerations before wrapping-up with a look at future trends of healthcare, big data, and analytics.

Chapter 3
Privacy & Safe Harbor

OVERVIEW

Safe Harbor is an interesting concept with numerous applications both inside the healthcare industry and beyond. In general, a safe harbor law states that certain types of behavior are not considered violations as long as they fall under a given rule, and those rules and regulations vary. We see Safe Harbor rules at the federal, state, county, and city levels alike.

Originally, "Rule 10B-18" of the "Securities Exchange Act of 1934" defined what would be called safe harbor laws.[19] As such, those new safe harbor laws would come to offer protection to people who were able to show "good faith" in their efforts.

Many years later, the ACA included a safe harbor designation with the goal of making employee healthcare coverage more affordable. More notably, the Department of Health and Human Services is proposing changes to the Stark Law and Anti-Kickback Statute to allow providers to coordinate care for a more value-based approach without running afoul of the law. For more information on those updates, please feel free to refer to this endnote.[20]

There's been a longstanding concern that current regulations may be unnecessarily and unfairly limiting the way providers coordinate their care (between other providers). Changes would allow for flexibility for innovation through outcome-based payment arrangements that reward improvements in a patient's health.

On the contrary, the newer, revised Stark Law will protect against overutilization and other harms, but the changes would offer specific safe harbors for coordinated care, value-based care, data sharing, and patient engagement activities.

For instance, a specialty physician practice could share data analytics services with a primary care physician practice. Or, a local hospital could improve its cybersecurity and the cybersecurity of nearby providers that it works with frequently. You see, many of the innovations we broached early on would not be possible without a safe harbor.

Hospitals and physicians are now able to work together in new ways to coordinate care for patients being discharged from the hospital. Meanwhile, hospitals can provide the patient's discharged info with care coordinators for follow-up care, data analytics, remote monitoring technology, alerts, etc, and so safe harbor with the new provision is a breakthrough in and of itself.

For example, a physician could provide what's called a "smart pillbox" to help their patients remember to take their medications on dose and on time. In fact, this "smart pillbox" could automatically alert a physician (or their personnel) or a caregiver if an important dose is missed, something with potentially life-changing implications.

To improve health outcomes for patients with end-stage diseases, for example, a provider could furnish their patients with technology capable of monitoring a patient's health with real-time interactive communication between all affected parties.

The proposed rules are part of HHS's Regulatory Sprint to Coordinated Care, which openly "seeks to promote value-based care by examining federal regulations that impede efforts among providers to better coordinate care for patients."[21] Furthermore, the proposed rule supports the agency's "Patients over Paperwork" initiative by reducing regulatory burdens and hopefully lowering costs.

The Stark Law has not been significantly updated since it was first enacted in 1989, which is important to note. At that time, healthcare was paid primarily on a fee-for-service basis, so volume was rewarded whether intentionally or not, but it did lead (one could Since the law was enacted back then, Medicare and the private market have implemented an array of value-based healthcare delivery and payment systems to address unsustainable cost growth in the current volume-based system, while the outdated Stark Law had not evolved to keep up with the changes.

Under that law, HIPAA protected data is now more sharable than ever. But isn't that a security and privacy issue? It could be. But if handled properly it will not become a widespread issue. At the same time, the issue of privacy is very nuanced. Let's discuss HIPAA as well as PI, PHI, and ePHI during the digital transformation. The PHI acronym stands for protected health

information. The Health Insurance Portability and Accountability Act (HIPAA) mandates that PHI in healthcare must be safeguarded. As such healthcare organizations must be aware of what is considered PHI.

HIPAA protected health information (PHI) is any piece of information in an individual's medical record that was created, used, or disclosed during the course of diagnosis or treatment that can be used to personally identify them. The meaning of PHI includes a wide variety of identifiers and different information recorded throughout the course of routine treatment and billing. Collecting PHI is a necessary component of the healthcare industry, and it needs to be attended to with the proper safeguards.

The following list includes every type of information that qualifies as HIPAA protected health information (PHI) identifiers according to guidance from the Department of Health and Human Services (HHS) Office for Civil Rights (OCR).[22]

Names. Addresses. Any dates (except years) that are directly related to an individual, including birthday, date of admission or discharge, date of death, or exact age of individuals over 89. Telephone numbers. Fax numbers. Email addresses. Web URLs. IP addresses. Account numbers. Certificate/license numbers. Medical record numbers. Social Security numbers. Health plan beneficiary numbers. Vehicle identifiers (i.e., license plate numbers, etc.). Device identifiers or serial numbers. Biometric identifiers (i.e., fingerprints, voiceprints, etc.). Full-face photos. Or, other unique identifiers, numbers, or codes.

PHI also extends to electronic records. In fact, it also has its own acronym. ePHI stands for "Electronic Protected Health Information," (ePHI) which translates into any PHI that is created, stored, transmitted, or received electronically. The HIPAA Security Rule has specific guidelines in place that dictate the means involved in assessing ePHI. This includes media used to store data such as personal computers with internal hard drives used at work, home, or while traveling. It also includes external portable hard drives, magnetic tape, removable storage devices, including USB drives, CDs, DVDs, and SD cards, and smartphones and PDAs. Means of transmitting data include wi-fi, Ethernet, modem, DSL, or cable network connections include email or any other means of file transfer.

PII is related to PHI and is also HIPAA protected.

PII & PHI

PII is an acronym standing for "Personally Identifiable Information." PII is HIPAA protected information (along with PHI). Namely, Titles II and III of the "E-Government Act of 2002" requires that agencies evaluate systems that collect personally identifiable information (PII) to determine that the privacy of this information is adequately protected.[23]

To ensure the info is adequately protected and thus meets the standards set forth under Titles II and III of the 2002 act, agencies must perform an assessment known as PIA or "Privacy Impact Assessment."

In accordance with HHS policy, operating divisions (OPDIVs) are responsible for completing and maintaining PIAs on all systems that are both in development and fully operational, an important distinction. Upon completion of each assessment, agencies are required to make PIAs publicly available, thus confirming their adherence to Titles II and III. If all this seems confusing, it's not.

PII or personally identifiable information is simply any data that can be used to contact, locate or identify a specific individual, either by itself or combined with other sources that are easily accessed. PII can include information that is linked to an individual through financial, medical, educational or employment records.

Some of the data elements that might be used to identify a certain person could consist of fingerprints or other biometric data, a name or something so simple as a telephone number or email address. The key is in safeguarding PII.

Though society has relied upon PII for some time, protecting it has become more important recently, mainly due to increased hacking scandals and the growing amounts of data in the healthcare space. Now that computer advances and technology improvements are taking place, the protection of PII is essential for organizations, as they store and/or attempt to analyze that information. Some of the laws that are related to different forms of

PII include HIPAA, the Privacy Act, GLBA, FERPA, COPPA, and FCRA.

Some examples of what may be identified as PII include a personal ID number (e.g. driver's license number, passport number, patient identification number, credit card number, social security number, etc.). A name, including the full name of the individual, their maiden name or mother's maiden name, and any alias they may use.

Also, asset information is PII, such as MAC address or IP, as well as other static identifiers that could consistently link a particular person. Address information like email addresses or street addresses is also PII.

Also, biological or personal characteristics, such as an image of distinguishing features, fingerprints, x-rays, voice signature, retina scan, or geometry of the face. Information about an individual that is linked to their place of birth is also PII.

Note, sometimes, under certain circumstances, one or two pieces of data can be brought together with other easily-accessible information to create a vulnerability for someone's identity. Even if the pieces of data seem to be harmless by themselves, if taken as a whole it can become PII and needs to be protected, as well.

HIPAA COMPLIANCE

HIPAA, or the Health insurance portability and accountability act, has required certain security regulations to be adopted for protected health information. Often, PHI is regarded to be any health information that is individually identifiable and created or received by a provider of health care, a health plan operator, or a health clearinghouse.

That information may relate to an individual's health (at any time). Generally, PHI is something that can be easily used to identify a specific individual, so if you ever have any questions of what is or isn't PHI, keep that in mind. Or, you may follow this link for additional information on PHI.[24]

Also note, there's a HIPAA Privacy Rule that provides federal protections for PHI that are held by Covered Entities (known as "CEs"), which gives patients' rights over their information.

More specifically, the Privacy Rule allows PHI to be disclosed as a result of patient care but has strict guidelines in place for maintaining the integrity and security of that information. There are specific measures within the rule requiring comprehensive administrative, physical, or technical safeguards that ensure the confidentiality, integrity, and security of PHI is met or exceeded.

It's important to note that HIPAA regulations actually treat data storage companies as Business Associates (BAs). The regulation accounts for the storage of physical and digital data, meaning that cloud storage services qualify as BAs even when the organization accesses or views the ePHI.

When dealing with data and cloud storage services, CEs and BAs must have Business Associate Agreements (BAAs) in place. A good BAA should include provisions that clearly delineate liability in the event of a data breach, in addition to the technical, administrative, and physical safeguards that can be put in place to maintain PHI or ePHI's integrity and security. Of course, the rules are even more nuanced and complex when we look at PI, PHI, and ePHI in terms of mental health.

PRIVACY & MENTAL HEALTH

The permitted uses and disclosures of PHI in the HIPAA Privacy Rule are critical components of a bill that was passed in 2016 known as the "Helping Families in Mental Health Crisis Act," which was signed into law as part of the "21ˢᵗ Century Cures Act" in December of that year. Congressman Tim Murphy backed the bill, saying that the "stigma surrounding mental illness" must end, with a key focus on patient care.

Prior to its passage, and after investigations, there apparently were findings that demonstrated fatal disconnections between 112 federal agencies concerning the mentally ill. In fact, billions of dollars were exposed as having been wasted as their efficacy came into question. However, members of both major parties came together at that time and passed the Helping Families in Mental Health Crisis Act" of 2016, which ensures better communications and adherence to HIPAA.

Ensuring a more compassionate communication on HIPAA regulations was a key aspect of the bill as well as clarifications necessary to the permitted uses and disclosures of patient's PHI data.

At the same time, as part of the research for this book, it came to my attention that the Privacy Rule does not allow healthcare organizations to treat patent records when an individual is being treated for mental health conditions. Providers are allowed to communicate with a patient's family, friends, and others in those circumstances.

For example, a provider can ask a patient's permission to share relevant info with family, or they may even tell a patient they plan to discuss their information and whether they permit or not. They may also utilize their best professional judgment as to whether a patient objects or not, something that may be particularly difficult in mental health situations.

Furthermore, the bills also explain whether or not there are development and dissemination of model training programs, something useful for our understanding herein. It clearly states that the Secretary must "identify or recognize private or public entities to develop model training and educational programs to educate healthcare providers, regulatory compliance staff, and others regarding the permitted use and disclosure of health information under HIPAA."

Improving leadership and accountability are also important aspects of the legislation. The bill also requires improved oversight of mental abuse and substance use disorder programs through what's known as the "Assistant Secretary for Planning and Evaluation" (or ASPE). And, it discusses how the federal government should promote access to mental health and substance use disorder care.

It is also now required for state prevention activities and responses to mental health and substance use disorder need to be properly supported. For more information on this bill, here's a helpful link in the endnotes.[25]

REVIEW & REFLECT

The key here is that privacy and patient security are mega important issues that must be solved if healthcare providers hope to reasonably take advantage of all the benefits of big data and predictive analytics. Some healthcare data has a long shelf life, and providers are legally required to keep patient data for at least six years.

As we've noted, the amount and efficacy of that data are of serious concern. As we look to future trends, we'll address more ways that analytics is reshaping the healthcare industry while helping to shift the ground beneath our feet. It's a particularly nuanced and complex area; feel free to refer to our endnotes and additional resources at your leisure.

As we look to ahead, preserving privacy and security while utilizing big data for the untold amounts of benefits it holds will be paramount as we find ways to transition to a more preventative health model.

Chapter 4

Identifying Trends

OVERVIEW

There are numerous trends in healthcare, many of which will have lasting impacts. As we wrap-up and pull things together, let's briefly review what we've covered plus take a shot at what all can be reasonably inferred as we look to the future. However, admittedly, it's impossible to completely predict the future of healthcare—or any industry.

We simply do not know what we do not know. However, analysts generally agree that there's a lot that can be gleaned from the mountains of data available. In fact, currently, as noted, there are about 2,300 exabytes of data just in the healthcare industry and it's growing exponentially each year.

If you stored that data on personal laptops then stacked them on top of one another, you would have a stack of computer that stretched 82,000 miles high, nearly one-third the way to the moon.

That's a lot of data.

Traditionally all that data has been viewed as problematic with all the storage, privacy, and security concerns it entails. Plus, about 80% of all that data is not being utilized at all. At the same time, practitioners are required by law to store information as it comes in for at least six years.

What if we could turn that mountain of a problem (pardon the pun) into a range of innovative solutions? Well, that's precisely what's occurring, particularly as we turn our eyes to the future of healthcare.

Take the citizens of the Netherlands for example. They now have access to one of the best healthcare systems in the world — and at reasonably affordable prices comparatively speaking. What's their secret?

Namely, Dutch health insurance companies must consistently monitor for fraud, waste, and abuse — all of which can raise insurance costs for everyone, and they're using big data and predictive analytics to do just that.

When it comes to costly incidents like fraud and abuse, early detection is the best remedy. We know that once claims are paid, it can be difficult if not impossible to get money back. It's the same way in how health services are rendered.

We can all agree that prevention is always better than curing something after the fact. But often companies and various stakeholders do not even communicate with each other.

That's why the goal of the Project Data Sphere initiative was to ignite innovation that will help the cancer community unlock the potential of valuable big data by creating all-new insights and opening up new research possibilities that were never before possible. Plus, the true power of the platform is derived from engaging the diverse, global community that's jointly committed to advancing future research and research opportunities in this critical area.

What if we made other initiatives and learned from Project Data Sphere or insurers in the Netherlands?

Marnix Suijkerbuijk, the Director of Health Care and Declaration Service at CZ believes we can. She said, "Through intelligent analysis, we can stay ahead of faulty statements and fraud."[26] CZ understood that it could uncover more fraud with analytics over a rules-based system alone, so they implemented SAS Detection and Investigation.

Their solution allows insurers to automate fraud discovery and check claims for fraud in real-time. Sophisticated data mining and extensive analysis With SAS Detection and Investigation, the Dutch health insurer now analyze health provider profiles more effectively. They use a comprehensive hybrid detection method that employs a combination of rules, anomaly detection, predictive models and social network analysis.

All this is particularly great news for analytics platforms in terms of payment integrity, member cost management, and healthcare fraud detection. Another interesting breakthrough is occurring with blockchain.

At its core, blockchain is a distributed system recording and storing transaction records, which makes it an ideal tool for healthcare providers, corporates, and other stakeholders.

The thing that makes blockchain so interesting is that its sharable and the immutable record of peer-to-peer transactions are built from linked transaction blocks then stored in digital ledgers. Blockchain relies on established crypto techniques taking a lot of the guessing game out of it, plus the fear of the unknown.

With blockchain, each participant in a network can interact (e.g. store, exchange, view, etc.), without preexisting trust between the two parties. Therefore, in a blockchain system, there are no central authorities or governing bodies; rather, transaction records are stored and distributed across all network participants. Because we have such clear-cut regulations in healthcare, it seems perplexing how to blend the two worlds.

Blockchain technology can be used to totally transform health care, placing the patient at the center of the health care ecosystem and increasing the security, privacy, and interoperability of health data. More specifically, it can provide a new model for health information exchanges (HIE) by making electronic medical records more efficient, disintermediated, and secure. While it is not yet a panacea, this new, rapidly changing industry is providing ample room for experimentation, investment, and proof-of-concept.

At the same time, blockchain technology is not fully mature today nor something that can be immediately applied. That's why several technical, organizational, and behavioral economic challenges must be addressed before a true healthcare blockchain can be adopted by organizations the world over.

However, we do understand that blockchain technologies create unique opportunities to reduce complexity, enable trustless collaboration, and create secure and immutable information being transferred, something that's key in the brave new world of 21st-century healthcare.

The opportunities to utilize blockchain to detect improper payments or healthcare fraud, for two examples, could be significant, which would lower costs across the board. Or, having an entire transaction/medical record and more information at hand than before would allow the advanced application of analytical methods for member cost and chronic condition management, which would have long-lasting reverberating implications.

From patient outcomes to payment integrity, blockchain heath data lends itself well to the application of analytics that can deliver insights in near-real-time to transform healthcare. Time will tell if we can take advantage of those opportunities, but my research leads me to believe we will.

In addition to blockchain, there are other important trends occurring in the industry. Firstly, we will continue to see a shift away from volume. Despite public opinion that might be to the contrary, healthcare providers are by and large At the same time, some providers have been a little bit resistant to take on risk, yet my gut says that they do recognize the potential to contain costs and improve quality of care overall.

As all this data assumes a central role in healthcare, the increasing availability of that data, the value that data represents, and the smarter integration of disconnected data systems will all make the transition easier and more scalable. Simultaneously, aptly named "big data" and predictive analytics is translating data into real health outcomes. And we've discussed IoT wearables, apps, and other technologies.

Big data and analytics have made significant advancements in making healthcare more technology-driven in recent years, and we can reasonably assume that trend to continue upward because a full, usable digital transformation hasn't even been fully realized yet. However, with the help of big data and smart analytics, we are finally at a point in healthcare where we can start making more accurate predictions in terms of possible complications, possible readmissions, the various outcomes of a care plan devised, and much more.

Not only it could big data and analytics translate to better health outcomes for the patients overall, as we've demonstrated, it could also spell out improvements in reimbursements and regulatory compliance, as well. Also, expect AI and IoT to take on a more central role. We've discussed these concepts already. Expect to see a great deal more investments from healthcare leaders in the fields of AI and IoT. As our own case study demonstrated, IoT has major implications that are already panning out nicely.

There is going to be a considerable advancement in technology, making the use of technology crucial in healthcare, while assisting the already unbalanced workforce. AI and IoT will prove instrumental in enhancing accuracy in clinical insights, security, privacy, and at limiting manual redundancy while ensuring fewer errors as we transition to a world of quality care (for the volume based on previously denoted).

Next, digital health interventions and virtual care are improving access and treatment. Some people thought wearables would die. I don't think so. The market is diversifying as clinical wearables gain importance and several renowned organizations integrate with each other.

Over the years, healthcare insurers have been stepping into the primary care delivery model, encouraging prevention and wellness to cut their own costs which are passed along to consumers. At the same time, we have witnessed a trend with hospitals and entire healthcare systems starting to go into the insurance space to take control of the complete patient care process. To those ends, expect to see continued merger activity. saw plus, hopefully, stabilizing healthcare costs.

Lastly, all the aforementioned trends will mean the increasing importance of security and privacy, some things we've also touched on. We deal with a tremendous amount of confidential and critical information in healthcare. It's not just patient health information, however. It goes from credit card information to digital footprints to the wide array of devices and systems storing information and more. The whole infrastructure is changing, while we're collecting more and more data all the time. Security and privacy will remain critical components of our entire healthcare system moving forward particularly as we shift away from the old preventive model.

There's a lot to be gleaned from data, and there's an almost infinite amount of it coming in all the time. We can remain in the dark ages in terms of data or start utilizing it for all it could spell out. It's impossible to say with 100% accuracy what all that might entail, but it's clear that we're heading in the right direction and that data and analytics will be a huge part of that.

As we analyze all the data it's leading to more and more breakthroughs, more and more insights, and denoting a massive shift away from the old, outdated, reactive healthcare system to one that's more reactive, predictive, and prescriptive. This new model is far more aligned with the changing needs of a growing population of people both domestically and abroad. For more information, please feel free to use the following additional resources.

Appendix

GLOSSARY

ACA: stands for "Affordable Care Act," which was the comprehensive health care reform law enacted in March 2010 with its three primary goals above others including to make affordable health insurance available to more people, provide consumers with subsidies, expand Medicaid to cover all adults with incomes below 138% of poverty, and support innovative medical care delivery methods designed to lower the costs of health care.

ACO: stands for "Accountable Care Organization," which is a network of physicians, hospitals, and other healthcare providers and suppliers that coordinate efficient, high-quality lower-cost care while sharing financial and medical responsibilities.

Artificial Intelligence (i.e., "AI" or "Machine Intelligence"): refers to the intelligence demonstrated by machines, which can emulate how human beings learn. AI can be defined as any device that perceives its environment and takes actions that maximize the chance of achieving goals (as in healthcare, finance, or other areas). For example, doctors can use machine intelligence to detect health problems early and actively diagnose in a more preventive healthcare model (versus reactive).

CARC: is an acronym for "Claim Adjustment Reason Codes," which are used to describe the reason for a payment adjustment relating to the adjudication of a healthcare claim.

CDT: an acronym for "Code on Dental Procedures and Nomenclature," which are used to document dental treatments.

Claims Data: includes demographics and other personal info, diagnostics, dates, costs and other billing info, a full range of traditional and non-traditional services (including at-home and ambulatory), all of which help providers process information and understand their patients' basic needs.

Claim Status Category Codes: these codes describe the general category of a claim's status (accepted, rejected, etc.).

CPT: an acronym for "Current Procedural Terminology" codes that are used for coding professional procedures (e.g., physician and outpatient). CPT codes are a HIPAA standard.

Descriptive Analytics: one of the four main categories of analytics. It helps analysts define or draw comparisons between two or more data sets and has been shown to be comprehensive, accurate, and effective.

Diagnostic Analytics: one of the four main categories of analytics, it can provide more information or pinpoint certain events as well as isolate information and drill-down to the root cause of an issue.

Disease Registries: clinical information systems that track a narrow range of key data for certain chronic conditions such as Alzheimer's Disease, cancer, diabetes, heart disease, and asthma.

DRG: stands for "Diagnosis Related Group," a grouping of patients who are anticipated to have similar needs, based on their diagnoses, treatments so far, and profiles in terms of age and prospective discharge date.

EHR: an acronym that standards for "Electronic Health Records." EHR provides many of the clinical clues that claim data often leaves out.

ePHI: an acronym standing for "electronically protected health information," which includes any PHI created, stored, transmitted, or received electronically.

EBM: stands for "Evidence-based Medicine," a big step in the right direction as we move forward. It's providing more help with simple hunches and helping practitioners determine what works best for the middle of a normal distribution of people.

HCPCS: an acronym for "Healthcare Common Procedure Coding System," which is used primarily to identify products, supplies, and services not included in the CPT code set (e.g., medical equipment, prosthetics, ambulance services, etc.).

HIE: an acronym standing for "Health Information Exchanges" that offer secure patient data storage within a specific care community. Many healthcare organizations have implemented or are in the process of working with private or public HIE solutions that enable numerous healthcare organizations to securely store and share medical data for their patients.

HIPAA: stands for the "Health Information Privacy and Portability Act," which is used by federal, state, county, other government sectors. HIPAA's Privacy Rule provided the first nationally recognized set of regulations concerning the use and/or disclosure of an individual's health and health care information.

HPTC: an acronym for "Healthcare Provider Taxonomy Codes," which categorizes the type, classification, and/or specialization of healthcare providers.

HRDRC: an acronym standing for "Healthcare Review Decision Reason Codes," which describes the reason for the health service review outcome.

ICD: stands for "International Classification of Diseases," which is coded data used by various healthcare providers and decision-makers to monitor the health of individuals and groups, as well as contribute to the analysis of the health system. Other ICD code data usages include hospitals, healthcare practitioners, government, professional associations, researchers, epidemiologists, academia (professors and students), and the general public.

ICD-10: the tenth revision of the International Statistical Classification of Diseases and Related Health Problems. ICD-10 is administered by WHO (World Health Organization).

LOINC: an acronym standing for "Logical Observation Identifiers Names and Codes," which are a universal standard used to assist in the electronic exchange and gathering of clinical information.

NUBC: an acronym standing for "National Uniform Billing Committee" code sets consisting of the following grains of data/codes and are used in or relating to healthcare claims.

PA: an acronym for "Predictive Analytics," which uses technology and statistical methods to search through massive amounts of information, analyzing it to predict outcomes for individual patients. That information can include data from past treatment outcomes as well as the latest medical research published in peer-reviewed journals and databases.

PDS: stands for "Project Data Sphere," a major global initiative that's igniting innovation that may help the cancer community unlock the potential of valuable big data by creating all-new insights and new research possibilities that were never before possible.

PGHD: stands for Patient Generated Health Data, which takes many forms including satisfaction surveys and patient-reported outcomes (PROs) as well as communications through portable, data streaming devices such as wearable fitness trackers and other Internet of Things (IoT) devices.

PHI: the acronym PHI stands for "protected health information" as it relates to HIPAA guidelines. PHI and ePHI (electronic PHI) are HIPAA protected.

PIA: stands for "Privacy Impact Assessment" which is used to ensure that info collected is adequately protected and thus meets the standards set forth under Titles II and III of the 2002 act.

PII: an acronym standing for Personally Identifiable Information. PII is HIPAA protected information. Some of the laws related to different forms of PII include HIPAA, the Privacy Act, GLBA, FERPA, COPPA, and FCRA.

Predictive Analytics: one of the four main categories of analytics, it helps analysts utilize historical and supplemental data to predict what may happen. Using that data and specific algorithms, they can determine the likelihood of a future event.

Prescriptive Analytics: one of the four main categories of analytics, it prescribes a solution to help manage a predicted event, and it involves applying advanced analytic techniques to make more informed decisions.

PSC: stands for "Place of Service Codes," which describes the location where a service is rendered.

RARC: stands for "Remittance Advice Remark Codes," which are used to further describe (in addition to the Claim Adjustment Reason Codes) the reason for an adjustment to claim payment or to or convey information about remittance processing.

SDoH: stands for "Social Determinants of Health." It can be used to augment existing analytics within an organization (i.e., income levels, reported behaviors, where an individual lives relative to access to care, grocery stores, or public transit, etc.).

Statistical Analysis System (i.e., "SAS"): developed by SAS Institute for advanced analytics, SAS software was developed first by NC State University from 1966 until 1976 and further developed in the 1980s and 1990s. SAS includes business intelligence applications as well as criminal investigations, data management, and predictive analytics in healthcare and other industries.

WHO: an acronym standing for World Health Organization. WHO manages healthcare data codes. Over time, the US (and other members) have altered codes to fit their needs.

ENDNOTES

[1]https://www.healthdataarchiver.com/health-data-volumes-skyrocket-legacy-data-archives-rise-hie/

[2]https://www.projectdatasphere.org/projectdatasphere/html/home

[3]https://www.sas.com/en_us/insights/articles/analytics/keeping-an-open-mind-about-open-analytics.html

[4]https://insights.principa.co.za/4-types-of-data-analytics-descriptive-diagnostic-predictive-prescriptive

[5]https://guides.lib.uw.edu/c.php?g=99209&p=642709#12207261

[6]https://healthitanalytics.com/news/which-healthcare-data-is-important-for-population-health-management

[7]https://www.cms.gov/About-CMS/Agency-Information/OMH/Downloads/CMS-Equity-Plan-for-Improving-Quality-in-Medicare-Report-2016.pdf

[8]https://www.healthit.gov/sites/default/files/medicationadherence_and_hit_issue_brief.pdf

[9]https://health.usnews.com/best-hospitals/area/oh/cleveland-clinic-6410670.

[10]https://www.sas.com/content/dam/SAS/en_us/doc/whitepaper1/emerging-topics-health-care-109815.pdf

[11]https://medium.com/google-cloud/tipping-your-toes-into-building-a-data-analytics-platform-on-gcp-2641926bc923

[12]https://www.cdc.gov/nchs/data/icd/uses_coded_clinicalinfosheet.pdf

[13]https://www.changehealthcare.com/support/customer-resources/hipaa-simplified/code-sets

[14]https://www.healthcare.gov/glossary/affordable-care-act/

[15]https://emerj.com/ai-sector-overviews/predictive-analytics-in-healthcare-current-applications-and-trends/

[16]https://www.apixio.com/case-studies/how-a-veteran-coder-used-apixios-hcc-profiler-to-eliminate-data-entry-error-and-double-productivity/

[17]https://www.sas.com/content/dam/SAS/en_us/doc/whitepaper1/emerging-topics-health-care-109815.pdf

[18]https://www.wearable-technologies.com/2018/10/the-state-of-wearable-technology-in-healthcare-current-and-future/

[19]www.upcounsel.com/safe-harbor-law

[20]https://www.hhs.gov/about/news/2019/10/09/hhs-proposes-stark-law-anti-kickback-statute-reforms.html

[21]https://www.healthcarefinancenews.com/news/hhs-and-cms-are-offering-safe-harbor-stark-law-promote-value-based-coordinated-care

[22]https://www.hipaajournal.com/considered-phi-hipaa/

[23]https://health.mil/Reference-Center/Forms

[24]https://www.hipaajournal.com/what-is-considered-protected-health-information-under-hipaa/

[25]https://healthitsecurity.com/news/considering-hipaa-privacy-rule-with-mental-health-data

[26]https://www.sas.com/en_us/customers/cz-nl.html